# FRUITS OF EXILE

By the same author:

*Proof* (2017)

# FRUITS OF EXILE

# MAGGIE SHAPLEY

RECENT
WORK
PRESS
2015-2025
10 YEARS OF POETRY

Fruits of Exile
Recent Work Press
Canberra, Australia

Copyright © Maggie Shapley, 2025

ISBN: 9781763670198 (paperback)

 A catalogue record for this book is available from the National Library of Australia

All rights reserved. This book is copyright. Except for private study, research, criticism or reviews as permitted under the Copyright Act, no part of this book may be reproduced, stored in a retrieval system, or transmitted in any form by any means without prior written permission. Enquiries should be addressed to the publisher.

Cover design: Recent Work Press
Set by Recent Work Press

recentworkpress.com
10 YEARS OF POETRY

*For my daughters*

# Contents

Introduction                                             1

## EMIGRATION (HELEN)
Leaving                                                  4
Arrival                                                  5
Travelling                                               6
Anniversary                                              7
Her grandchild                                           8
Zoom                                                     9

## MARRIAGE (LIZ)
Nightfall                                               12
Dream                                                   13
Duty statement                                          14
Her sister                                              15
Marriage                                                16
Blue-stocking                                           17
Burning Sappho                                          18

## CHILDREN (TRISH)
Her father's house                                      22
Her husband                                             23
Children                                                24
Tuckshop duty                                           25
Old flame                                               26
Return                                                  27
Fruits of exile                                         28

## LEAVING (MEG)
Driving home                                            32
Post-natal                                              33
The reason                                              34
Last night                                              35

| | |
|---|---:|
| Leaving | 36 |
| Exile | 37 |
| Dinner parties | 38 |

## MISOGYNY (FRAN)

| | |
|---|---:|
| Mending | 42 |
| Her mother | 43 |
| The other world | 44 |
| Grief | 45 |
| Fifty ways | 46 |
| Unfinished business | 47 |
| Football | 48 |

## ALIENATION (LINDA)

| | |
|---|---:|
| Washing up | 52 |
| Her grandmother | 53 |
| Musician | 54 |
| Migration | 55 |
| Piano | 56 |
| Collected Poems | 57 |

## DOMESTICITY (JESS)

| | |
|---|---:|
| Driving home | 60 |
| Marriage | 61 |
| Mansplaining | 62 |
| Housework | 63 |
| Coercive control | 64 |
| Breaking | 65 |
| Decision | 66 |

# Introduction

A book club is meeting at the home of Linda and Tom in Canberra. Usually the group are all women but tonight Jess is accompanied by her partner, Peter, so Tom joins in as well. The participants:

**Helen** was born in England and is a 75-year-old widow.
**Liz** is a poet and teacher in her mid-fifties.
**Trish** is married, now retired and in her early seventies.
**Meg** is married and in her late fifties.
**Fran** came to Australia as a child, is single and 48 years old.
**Linda**, 60, is an editor and emigrated as a child from Germany.
**Jess** is an accountant in her early thirties and married to Peter.
**Peter** is a public servant in his mid-thirties and married to Jess.
**Tom** is married to Linda and is in his sixties.

On this occasion, the book club discusses the work of poets Gwen Harwood and Margaret Scott and in particular their poems on the theme of exile. Extracts from the discussion over the course of several hours are interspersed with poems relating to the seven women who are there, some reflecting their reactions to the conversation and to the poems discussed and others elucidating their past and, in some cases, their future lives.

Quotations from poems by Gwen Harwood and Margaret Scott are indicated by italic font in the poems and the source poems are identified at the end of the work, along with references to the poems discussed and other notes.

# EMIGRATION (HELEN)

| | |
|---|---|
| Linda | Let's start with Margaret Scott's poems about coming to Australia. |
| Meg | Imagine that journey from Cambridge to Hobart! She knew Ted Hughes and Sylvia Plath, was even at the party where they met and kissed. |
| Jess | Then why come here? |
| Peter | Maybe she was recruited there and sent to Hobart—a Soviet spy for the Antipodes? |
| Liz | No, it's the old story, Jess—her husband's job and she was pregnant—before the Pill, women didn't get much choice. |
| Linda | This isn't Stitch 'n Bitch—what about the poems? 'In Tasmania', for example? |
| Liz | Well, the rhyming couplets and simple words undercut the promise—'so like England'—at the start, then the deadpan rhythm 'no end of days' ... |
| Helen | That's how I felt when I arrived here—'strange as the cold face of a passer-by'. Everything was foreign, even the light. |
| Linda | And 'peculiar birds' is perfect—the first time I heard a kookaburra!—and Scott arrived in summer to dead grass. |
| Peter | Which poem is this? |
| Linda | We've moved on to 'Migrants'—'stripped of custom, friends and art'. |
| Helen | And in 'North to South'—you're shedding everything and everyone you've ever known. |
| Fran | I was an innocent—I remember my mother holding me up to the tiny porthole in our cabin. |
| Trish | I've never even left Australia. |
| Tom | Me neither, nor Gwen Harwood. |
| Linda | Yes, Tasmania was her foreign country. |

# Leaving

She couldn't remember deciding to leave—
it was more just going along with his plans,
the spiralling list of things to organise,
the helter-skelter of family visits, then
crossing things off one-by-one
and bracing for the next activity,
until it was too late to have an opinion—
the forms signed off, the farewell now arranged.
Suddenly *the liner looms from the wharf,*
the coast stretches wide, and all she's known
sinks from sight, swamped by roiling sea.
Against the deluge, she seizes his arm,
her sailor's grip firm around his wrist,
tight panic in her whispered 'save me'.

# Arrival

She wasn't prepared for the informality
and casual confidence of 'she'll be right',

a child saying 'she sounds just like the Queen'—
but no one cut her dead in the high street

or implied she'd married above her station.
In letters home, she underplayed her hand,

didn't boast about her husband's promotion,
their palatial house above the bay,

in that *texture of strangeness everywhere.*

# Travelling

They'd always planned to travel together—
once the children had grown with steady jobs,
once they'd paid off their first house,
once he had that longed-for promotion,
once the nest egg grew.

She found the box clearing out his study—
their folder 'Where to go' bulged with ideas,
its covers outgrown with postcards from old friends,
pages torn from Lonely Planet guides.
'It's time', she thought, 'only first class will do'.

# Anniversary

He'd been gone for twenty years
but still they chatted over morning coffee.
It wasn't wasted, the second cup—
how else to conjure up his voice
and see how he warmed his fingertips
as she read aloud the crossword clues.

'Yes, of course, that's it!' she'd say—
he would invariably agree, of course—
through *the shielding leaves of memory*
it was her way to stall forgetfulness,
sweeping debris from neural pathways,
filling absence with found, familiar words.

# Her grandchild

With the arrival of her first grandchild
she thought she'd be the family babysitter,
but after the happy snaps as proud grandmother,
her expertise was suddenly out-of-date,
and when her daughter moved to distant Melbourne—
it was as if payback for what she'd done
to her own mother, leaving her in England—
a retribution arriving fashionably late.
Now she waits for an invitation, phoning
to hear the recorded 'please leave a message',
*waltzing the edge between a bright pretence*
*and speechless words* for the thwarting of love.

# Zoom

Her daughter left home and moved away
before FaceTime, or Skype, or Zoom—
all just a Jetsons gimmick back then.

Now, the technology's novelty has faded
after months of exile—no touching of hands,
or perfume's scent, or eloquence

of held embraces. She waves goodbye to the screen,
zooms back to her empty house, remembers
the old anticipation of the mail—

the slicing of the envelope, unfolding
the tightened creases, her daughter's handwriting
on flimsy paper, right there in her hand.

# MARRIAGE
# (LIZ)

| | |
|---|---|
| Linda | How about '1945' as a title? Liz—you're the poet—is that unusual? |
| Liz | She's just making a point. It's when Harwood married—a watershed, but published much later. |
| Jess | Like a Google review forty years too late. |
| Peter | She complains it's cold—it's Tasmania—like Queenslanders at the airport in shorts and thongs. |
| Fran | It's the metaphorical 'cold shoulder', the waitress saying, 'Lunch is off'. |
| Trish | It's like any country town. |
| Liz | Hobart was unsophisticated—imagine getting a coffee then. Impossible! |
| Linda | I'm struck by her mask—she's devastated, but says 'how charming'. She doesn't go back home for twenty years. |
| Jess | She's unhappy but she stays? Why doesn't she leave? |
| Meg | Her husband's job demanded it. Like Scott, she lives in Tasmania the rest of her life. |
| Helen | Is that so strange? I've been here fifty years. |
| Tom | That poem, 'Suburban Sonnet'—she's disillusioned, trying to play Bach, the milk's boiling over, the kids are arcing up … |
| Meg | Yes, 'tasty dishes from stale bread'—she might as well have said 'the honeymoon's over'. |
| Liz | In 'Burning Sappho' she simply wants an hour to herself. |

# Nightfall

Colour dissolves to shadow.
From the kitchen window, city lights,
the café where poets sit with their drinks
for open mic and obligatory applause.
Her notebook's propped behind the taps
and she reads aloud, alert for dissonance
or the awkward word, stores amendments
(move that phrase, ditch that line). Word perfect,
she peels off her adhesive rubber gloves—
the plates are squeaky-clean, the glasses sparkling.

# Dream

She's chasing a dream as she wakes,
catching its coat-tails if she can—
some detail of landscape, the furniture:
a giant flashing screen, a TV quiz,
a cryptic crossword and every answer's a poem.
She's in luck—she recognises the poet—
the first clue's 'Navigating one's mind?'
'I am Captain of My Soul' she shouts.
Now she's the compere and the subject's trivia:
that know-all's chosen famous Australians.
Ten cricketers who aren't Don Bradman?
Easy peasy. Ten female poets
who aren't Judith Wright? Gotcha moment.

## Duty statement

Serve all members of the household, viz:

1. Shop for meat, fish and various miscellanies
2. Cook meals, catering for all intolerances
3. Wash dishes, glassware and cutlery (shine every finger mark into a polish)
4. Wash and iron business shirts, school uniforms and lingerie
5. Attend to dogs, cats, chickens, rabbits, rats and mice
6. Maintain the cleanliness and sanitation of the home — dust, polish, sweep, vacuum, mop, spray, wipe, scrub and disinfect
7. In the event of business trips, mow the lawn and then put out the garbage.

Apply within. A wedding ring provided.

# Her sister

There's been a systemic failure—the accountant's here
to follow the money. Her sister listens closely:
So let me get this right, this work as listed,
you agreed to do, seven days a week
and no particular sign-off 'until bedtime'—
unpaid, not counting reimbursement
of household expenditure, and let's call them gifts—
a winter coat, some jewellery and maybe four
good dresses over the years. In return
you transferred your savings to his account
to offset the mortgage—yes, I'm aware
of the interest-saving potential—
and now your husband has passed on—
my condolences, sorry for your loss—
and left his house to his son by a previous marriage,
you'd like to know if you would have been
better off to divorce him while you could?
Well, let's consider any remaining options,
*the world that was the case already* gone.

# Marriage

Harwood disguises her discontent
behind pseudonyms, but metaphors
betray her: *Where's the demon lover—*
*who swore to love her through hell's own fires?*
*In warm thighs a fleshless devil*
*chops him to bits with hell-cold evil.*
In public, she's someone's kindly, forgiving aunt,
her white, peaked collar neatly pressed,
vowing to *be faithful to the last,*
*an old blind dog that knows the stairs.*
You should never trust a poet,
they're such eloquent and unseemly liars.

# Blue-stocking

The acid-tongued Alexander Pope
dismissed a female poet with disparaging words:
'a blue-stocking with an itch for scribbling'.

Thanks for your encouragement, learned sir,
an inspiration for every 'poetess'
to change her name to something masculine
or more ambiguous, perhaps initials.

When Walter Lehmann signed off her poems,
Harwood's rejection slips stopped dead
(ditto Francis Geyer and Timothy Kline).
What magic power was in those names
not already sparking in her poems?

# Burning Sappho

When Liz left her marriage, her friends called
her brave, or did that mean foolhardy?
No one ever says you're brave to signal
for the lifeguard when you're drowning.

Burning Sappho wants to leave but fails,
there's always some crisis or excuse for staying on
and then she's side-stepped her chance again.

Where's the woman who swore to *find my truth,*
*my poem, and grasp it yet,* who'd rather be
a bag lady by the turbulent Brisbane River?
Her ashes were given to the brackish tide.

# CHILDREN (TRISH)

| | |
|---|---|
| Linda | So they both wrote 'Return of the Native' poems … |
| Peter | We had to read that novel at school. Is it relevant to these poems? |
| Liz | No, not really. Scott's ambivalence is clear, but is Harwood's nostalgia genuine? For instance, when she says 'The last camphor laurel cut down, alas'. |
| Fran | Scott's family treats her like a foreigner: 'There were too many like her nowadays in his country, throwing their money about'. |
| Helen | And in 'Return to Tockington' she complains, 'life's sailed on without me'. |
| Trish | When I went back to where I'd grown up it was bizarre – huge rooms had shrunk to normal size and all the streets had narrowed. |
| Meg | 'Everything I love's Down Under now': a very English way to say it—she's thinking of going home to her children. |
| Linda | But what about 'Fruits of Exile', where she's estranged from them because they're Australian? She says, 'my legacy falls to dust'. |
| Helen | They both discover the place, or house, isn't what's important —it's the people. |
| Liz | Nice idea, but read Harwood's biography—her kids leave home but she never entirely gives up on getting back to Brisbane. |

# Her father's house

In her father's house, breakfast was at eight
and began with the Bible. Sunday was set aside
for church and inward contemplation.
If she had opinions, she was wilful,
if she answered back, then insolent,
and sent to her father's study for instruction.
She'd let his words bounce around the bookshelves,
keeping her thoughts safe from correction.
Behind glazed eyes, she'd repeat her mantras:
'be of good cheer' and 'time heals even this'.
She caught the train after her exams were over,
leaving his house, against all insistence.

# Her husband

When she talked with friends, she realised
it was a kind of lottery she'd won—
she didn't have sad stories of his conduct
or how he reacted to bitter accusations.
There were no hidden secrets, or purpling bruises.
Instead, they revelled in conversation,
disagreed with wit, loved to plan
projects, trips together and separately,
delighting in company and in solitude.
She knew he was a keeper when he said,
'do what's right for you—there are no rules'.

# Children

'Back then, you had to have them, no choice.
Abstinence wasn't a popular option
and birth control a kind of guessing game.
If you breastfed and rode your luck,
you could keep them two years apart—
not counting twins—until the necessity
of brutal hysterectomy.' Trish knew
as she said it, she'd not said the worst:
*small yellow face, silent grin,*
*pearlskull, frog-pale fingers spread,*
*the still centre of spinning light,*
the unnamed one, only briefly seen.

# Tuckshop duty

On tuckshop duty she bit her tongue,
abstained from the banter of the pack—
its rehash of talk-back radio, first-world slights
puffed up to deliberate provocation—
what poisonous privilege were they serving up
with chicken nuggets and dipping sauce?

She spread the butter carefully on fresh-cut bread,
was generous with tomato, lettuce, cheese,
then extra grated carrot, a pinch of salt,
crafting her antidote for all the world's ills.

# Old flame

She'd beaten him in every subject,
her dux's medal in a box somewhere,
but he now wore the suit in a corner office
with a wide view and his own p.a.,
his wife's photo on a tidy desk—
the partner he'd long since left her for,
who'd come from money and would never
outshine him or insist on a career.
Trish is applying for a part-time job—
school-hours only, well beneath her grade.
He smiles, and asks, 'What have you been doing?'—
gazing with the eyes she once adored.
'Three children? Yes, me too', he says,
as if there were a simple equivalence,
as if she would forgive the lower pay.

# Return

What she remembers as vast—waiting at its edge
for the daily roll-call—is a small yard under trees
and a row of bubblers hugging the cracking asphalt.
The steep, wide stairs where she'd cut her head
are shallow steps, and the grey weatherboard house
is closed in by verandas. Main-street shops
are boarded-up, and the bank's façade
offers a window to an ATM.
She half-expects someone to call the name
she hasn't used for fifty years, but only
the silence speaks of the familiar now alien.

# Fruits of exile

The Sunday night roast was her specialty,
she knew the timings from sight and smell,

peeling potatoes and slicing up a pumpkin,
saving the seeds to plant out in spring.

If there were peas to pod or beans to slice
she'd do that next: steam gently, do not boil.

Don't start the gravy until the meat is resting,
using the juice—then mint sauce for the peas.

After her children left, they'd often find
their way back on a Sunday. Now she's googling,

'tasty snacks' and 'fat-free vegan meals'.

# LEAVING (MEG)

Linda     How about Harwood's 'In the Park'?

Jess     I remember that from school—the cartoon balloon above his head and how she pretends everything is fine until the final line.

Peter     Her children have 'eaten her alive'—how's that possible?

Linda     Think hyperbole. Consuming all her time and energy, what's left for her?

Trish     Or you could take it literally—she's 'nursing the youngest child'. It could mean breastfeeding.

Fran     How dare she complain—her choice. She didn't have to have them!

Trish     You don't know until you've had them, and then you can't just 'return to sender'.

Meg     I recognised it instantly—the way they take you over.

Liz     But it's not Harwood—just a character. Every time she was asked, she said, 'are my clothes shabby and old-fashioned? Did Coleridge shoot an albatross? No!'

Meg     Of course it's her—as if a man could have written that.

Trish     All mothers know it's true, but it's rarely said out loud.

Helen     You survive, and she regretted saying it: 'She sits in the park, wishing she'd never written about that dowdy housewife'.

# Driving home

So many things, small and large—
no spare time to read the newspaper,
the green two-seater sportscar
with stitched upholstery—sold,
her study turned into the nursery,
her framed degrees stuffed into the shed,
her books went there as well, and then her desk
became a change-table, never to change back.
She turns up Mozart to block out children's songs:
'We're going on a bear hunt, I'm not scared'.

# Post-natal

The doctor suggested she ask her husband to help,
'perhaps some leave to give you a chance to rest?'
She nodded and paid the bill, edged the pram
around the waiting room's tight corners,
avoiding the watching eyes, sat at the bus-stop,
dog-tired, and began to sob.
Her four-year-old gently patted her arm:
'There, there,' she said, 'all better now'.
'Where did you learn to say that?' Meg laughed,
wiping her tears on her sleeve. Of course, from her—
the daughter becoming mother to the mother.

# The reason

It was not, so much, his occasional disloyalty
or how he watched the football endlessly
while refusing to share the household load.
It was more his future retirement plans
requiring her active participation:
eighteen holes of golf twice a week
and Friday nights ensconced within the clubhouse.
She teed up as fast as she was able—
a deliberate hook into the distant rough—
and found another club—no joining fees—
where people read books and exercised their minds,
forfeiting the chicken parma and thin beer.

# Last night

She'd come prepared with a tawdry, false confession
to counter his 'I'm begging you to stay'—
or would he try, 'we're soul-mates', yet again?

Now, another round. She'd made sure
no one would interrupt, messaging a friend:
'I'll contact you by nine'. But, in the end,

a non-event—her opponent lay down his arms,
wanting to know when she was moving out.

# Leaving

In the absence of others,
she says goodbye to a tree.
Places both her hands against the trunk,
looks up into the canopy of green,
and lets her body weight fall forwards
onto its bark—it holds her there,
leaving its roughness imprinted in skin.
She'd witnessed its growth from stick-like sapling:
it was time for remembering
how far they'd both come.

# Exile

That first weekend—her own place,
out on the deck—hot, still night,
infinite stars, a glass of red.
No one joins her or calls her in.
She watches bright eyes meet hers
through a sheltering grapevine—
a possum cradles a purple fig.
She opens her ears
to the enormous silence
and drinks it in.

# Dinner parties

Dinner parties became a scene of ambush.
She'd find herself paired with eligible men—
divorced, widowed or, sometimes, never married—
suggesting a movie or tomorrow's concert.
Occasionally she'd go, as a way of checking
whether she'd been too quick in her escape,
but they would mirror their own loss,
regaling her with their side of sadness—
as if she offered some kind of solution.
She thought about a lonely-hearts ad:
'Self-sufficiency seeks the same,
view companionship—but never for sale'.

# MISOGYNY
# (FRAN)

Linda    So what's next—time for more of Margaret Scott?

Liz    How about the witches? She planned six more, including one about Medea.

Fran    I could hardly bear to read these poems—what these women were up against.

Trish    'Thou shalt not suffer a witch to live', the Bible says, but who decides who is one? The men in charge, that's who.

Liz    For misogynists like John Knox it was all about intimidating women …

Peter    It wasn't just misogynists—I'm not defending them—but men were also tried and executed, in their thousands.

Fran    But mostly women, yes? Hundreds of thousands falsely accused.

Peter    That's not right, no way—Wikipedia says thirty-five thousand.

Linda    Scott captures the injustice, making it up close and personal.

Trish    An impossible choice—confess to find 'favour' but if you don't you 'shall surely burn and hang'.

Meg    Like the ducking stools—if you floated you were a witch—if you sank, innocent, except you'd likely drown.

Jess    Really? That's crazy.

Fran    Exactly. But Scott has an alternative history—the good witch who saves Hansel and Gretel.

# Mending

She'd ripped her jacket in her haste to leave.
Now she sat, her needle flashing in
and out of black velvet *making a seam,*
*a dark line like a straight creek*
containing her rage. His insistence that men
were also targeted—no doubt he'd say
'women can also be the perpetrators
of domestic violence' and 'I'm no misogynist'.
She wished she'd said: 'they were real women,
every one, destroyed by trumped-up charges—
those who knew too much, or owned good land,
or were simply in the way, or wouldn't
obey the rules imposed by men, intended
to keep them cowed and silent. Just like me.'

# Her mother

Her mother's secrets were not to be revealed—
she'd told her 'just between us two'—
why they'd moved half a world away,
her fiction about a freak accident,
to explain away the absent husband and father,
why they moved again, to another town,
to escape the one who'd said he'd keep them safe.
That night, her mother had promised 'a new adventure',
carried her to the car bundled in blankets,
with a clutch of books. She heard the thump
of her mother's chest, as if rebounding
from the moon-bleached streets, while
raking headlights caught her mother's tears,
bright as unlikely starbursts.

# The other world

She has few memories of that other place:
a cottage close to a wooded hill, fruit trees,
vegetable patch, a cluck of hens, a cat.
Her mother gathered for the preserving jars,
they knew the wild herbs and salad greens,
birds and woodland creatures and the seasons—
until the night they heard *the window thump
and shatter like an icy wave breaking.*

# Grief

When her mother died, grief arrived
uninvited, sat in her mother's chair
recounting things she'd said, half-remembered—
'remember when' they'd begin, 'when you
were just a child', then the tears and regret,
'I should have asked her that before she went'.

It took some weeks until 'needs must':
the clothes washed and ironed, carefully folded,
each garment laid in black plastic bags,
the vases emptied, the spring bulbs waiting.

# Fifty ways

When he finally answers his phone, Paul Simon
is background rhyming noise. She hears,

distorted into squawks and fuzzy static,
'there must be fifty ways to leave your lover'.

Yesterday she'd gathered his clothes and books,
scanned each room for treasures to relinquish,

gently brushed his coat, as if he wore it,
filled five cardboard boxes. She says,

'They're on the step, although it looks like rain.'
Yes, she thought, there must be fifty ways,

but you only need the one,
and it doesn't have to rhyme with anything.

# Unfinished business

The lovers, like frost-tender seedlings,
needing warm air and sunlight to thrive:
that season has gone, the now-or-never urgency,
the coming alive at the witching hour.

The children she didn't have, the grandchildren
she never told her stories of growing up:
the midnight adventures, the years of hiding.

The father who kept his mystery,
allowing the possibility of redemption,
as much as drunken brawl or overdose
or sentenced to life for unspeakable crimes.

# Football

She may be lucky today, no sense
of shadows of others of her kind,
she may have the game to herself.
She checks the players as they run on—
who will be her chosen one?
Who on the news will 'blitz the field'
or 'pull off the magic pass',
who will be crowned 'man of the match'
by those deluded commentators?
She has her man and he has the ball—
she harnesses the tribal will—
repeats the spell again and again.
She steps away from the cheers of the crowd
and holds their pleasure close inside.

# ALIENATION (LINDA)

| | |
|---|---|
| Linda | These poems about Professor Kröte … |
| Trish | I don't understand them. Why write about a guy who's always drunk? |
| Fran | And moody, malicious, a 'gross buffoon'. |
| Tom | I googled Kröte—it's 'toad' in German. |
| Liz | He's a device, isn't he, personifying alienation? |
| Trish | Why does he drink red wine at the beach? Like he's deliberately not fitting in. |
| Linda | He's European. There, you rent a deckchair, order drinks from the bar. Here, he's attacked by a child and mother-shamed as a 'filthy pervert'. |
| Trish | Should we be sympathetic then? |
| Helen | And he's a composer who talks about Brahms and Liszt—is that rhyming slang? Harwood's joke? |
| Jess | 'The Silver Swan' was devastating—his brilliant student becomes 'this shabby housewife'. |
| Liz | Some of these were published in *The Bulletin* … |
| Meg | Didn't they publish those sonnets that said 'Fuck all editors'? |
| Liz | Yes, she hoaxed them with hidden acrostics and a male pseudonym—they'd rejected her poems for years but her male brilliance caught the editor's eye. |

# Washing up

'Why did Peter insist on coming tonight?'
asks Linda, 'has he ever read a poem?
Does he realise Cambridge is a university
and not a spy factory? Honestly!'
'I've no idea what's going on,' says Helen,
'but it's like he's trying to shut Jess down.
And did you see his face when she asked
why Harwood didn't leave? As if the thought
had never entered his teeny-tiny brain'.

# Her grandmother

At the first concert of the season,
three rose-cut diamonds flash their light—
the young soprano, swathed in satin folds,
summons Bach cantatas centre-stage,
*the fullness of all passion* in rounded vowels,
corralled by crisp German consonants.
Linda is taken back to her grandmother's house,
allowed to stay up late, the drawing room
with red velvet chairs and gold-plaited
braid swagging back heavy curtains,
glittering dresses and tall black suits swirl
around the parquet floor. Her grandmother
smiles and adjusts the violin under her chin,
*music, my joy* circling overhead.

# Musician

She's *a child blessed with perfect pitch,*
her grandmother proudly told her friends.
Not blessed, but cursed, *the noise is fearful,*
the school piano's horribly out of tune—
she can hardly bear to play the notes,
like fingernails scraping a blackboard,
but the whole school stands watching—
the national anthem must be played right through.
She recollects that day, and the migraine's pain,
knows the torment of *senseless noise, the howling,*
the constant search for a true harmony.

# Migration

She learnt quickly when she went to school
to always speak English, but her name and accent
labelled her as other. When she married
she took Tom's name, happy to accept one
that people could pronounce. Last week she read
her old name scrawled inside a schoolbook—
who was that imposter claiming her identity?
She saw the classroom lit with brilliant summer,
the teacher taking the roll, and sniggering students,
and felt herself blush, remembering the old coastline
where fishermen brought shiny *Sardinen*
from the Baltic sea into the market.

# Piano

When Linda read how Harwood said,
she'd happily become a passive listener
rather than practising musician,
that listening soothed her feelings of exile,
she knew she was straight-out lying.
How impossible when muscle memory
tells you 'play', how your fingers ache
when you hear the familiar, ringing notes.
For Linda, the voyage out was hell,
and for Harwood, years of straitening discord,
until she accepted a friend's offer,
challenging her husband's indifference,
installing the beast—the piano—in the lounge.

# Collected Poems

Jess has the *Collected Poems:*
edges spiked with post-it notes,
highlighted in pink and blue—
she wants to read aloud her favourites.
Linda thinks it'll take till midnight,
and iambics are not for everyone,
suggests that Jess give her voice a break.

Remembering how Harwood liked
to dissemble, to impishly insert
what she called her 'double octaves'
to throw interviewers off the scent,
Linda skips every second post-it.
So long, *Collected Poems*,
praise be to all editors.

# DOMESTICITY
# (JESS)

| | |
|---|---|
| Linda | Let's end with Scott's housework poems. The early ones satiric but then she embraces the subject. |
| Meg | Yes, 'Housewife' is all about surfaces—and I don't just mean the Laminex. The domestic veneer hides oppression. |
| Trish | I think she's saying that way madness lies—the jars are grinning and the refrigerator's shrieking. |
| Meg | 'The floor was scrubbed. The windows shone'. That reminds me of Harwood's, 'The clothes are washed, the house is clean'. These women are constantly dealing with hidden menace. |
| Jess | They sound like Stepford Wives. In 'Tea Party'—'the ladies in their linen frocks shed little showers of twinkling words'—so much is polite and superficial. |
| Fran | It's like a movie, how it cuts to close-up—the 'old hand with heavy rings'. |
| Liz | But doesn't 'foil scraps of words' being 'forged' sound contrived? |
| Linda | The later housework poems seem to celebrate the domestic … |
| Jess | She lost me there—who'd polish a step? |
| Helen | She's making a point about women being bonded through sharing the same tasks over time. |
| Peter | But washing's easy now—you just throw the clothes in the machine—why would you write a poem about that? |
| Tom | It does sound sentimental: 'chaos defeated again, a clean sheet', but I agree with Jess, polishing a step is ridiculous. |
| Liz | She's claiming women's work as worthy of poetry—enough already of poems about cricket or football or birds. |
| Fran | I like 'labouring since the time that pots were fired'—that sense of continuity over millenia. |

# Driving home

'So that was interesting,' he said and she agreed,
fell right in, too tired to read the sneer.
'You didn't have to come,' she dared,
'I thought you wanted to meet my friends'—
cut off—'What use are they to me?'
Pull back, she thought, just let that slide.
After two years it was not as she'd imagined—
the cooking together, wine and conversation
they'd both enjoyed when dating for a year.
How quickly they'd slipped into other patterns:
while she cooked, he'd drink and scroll through Netflix,
and then she'd read to escape the noise.
Those poets—older than her grandmother—
knew what it was like. How well they knew.

# Marriage

It suited him to move and so they did—
her accountancy business could flourish anywhere.

The next winter it snowed—the lemon tree
she'd brought with her wilted in the frost.

She'd sold her apartment to help finance this house
and agreed on a joint account. Now her mother's

words returned: 'you need a separate fund
for running-away'—she'd thought it was a joke.

Outside, the wind off the Snowies blew
dark autumn leaves, *cold truth* lay on the lawn.

# Mansplaining

He's explaining
what she should do next,
in precise detail,
without pause or interruption—
an envelope of sound.

At first, his voice on her skin
was like a summer shower,
washing grit from foliage.
Now, a dripping tap
pounds in her brain.

# Housework

'Clean house—wasted life'
had always been her mantra.
Kept things tidy, in their place,
avoiding known health hazards—

she'd wipe the benches, mop
the kitchen floor, and vacuum
for dust mites, but had no need
for silver polish or extra sparkle.

Then his mother's visit, bringing with her
handy hints and the all-purpose spray.
Yes, she agreed with his suggestion—
'just an hour a day'. Why not you?

# Coercive control

'How much did that cost?' is how it starts.
That first time she tells him, he crimps her wings.
She learns to fabricate and douse displeasure
with soothing clucking words, her doublespeak.

How does it end? The receipts are already shredded
and feeding the worms. When it's tax time,
he'll discover payback: her neat rows
and columns add up to something else.

# Breaking

He'd corner her in the kitchen
as if it were the natural place as site
of her culinary and domestic failures.
She'd brace against the cutlery drawer—
its sharp contents became her whitest fear—
but cups and glasses were easy missiles, creating
their own havoc. Where was the evidence?
What proof he'd ever laid a finger on her?
Except now, relaxed with friends at a bar,
at the sudden crash of breaking glass,
she's out of her seat, white-faced, trembling,
wide-eyed, and fumbling to open the door.

# Decision

Someone has made a decision
but you don't know it yet.
They've signed a lease, gathered
cash in a separate account,
made a list of what they're taking,
written a three-page explanation.
When you get home from work
it's there ice-cold on the kitchen table.
You recognise the handwriting and wonder
where she is, what's happened,
why she's written a letter.
Perhaps she's changed her mind
about starting a family,
needs your reassurance,
is asking for forgiveness
for yesterday's argument,
but it's none of that,
not even close.

# References

### EMIGRATION

Scott: 'In Tasmania', 'Migrants', 'North to South'. All quotations from Margaret Scott, *Collected Poems* (Montpelier Press: Dynnyrne Tas., 2000).

'Leaving'—Scott: 'North to South'

'Arrival'—Scott: 'Migrants'

'Anniversary'—Scott: 'Migrants'

'Her grandchild'—Scott: 'North to South'


### MARRIAGE

Harwood: '1945', 'Suburban Sonnet', 'Burning Sappho'. All quotations from Alison Hoddinott and Gregory Kratzmann (eds), *Gwen Harwood: Collected poems* (UQP: St Lucia Qld, 2003).

'Nightfall' is the title or first word of several of Harwood's poems; the last line mirrors the first line of 'Burning Sappho': 'The clothes are washed, the house is clean'.

'Dream'—refers to Harwood's poem 'I am Captain of My Soul'.

'Her sister'—Harwood: '1945'

'Marriage'—Harwood: 'Suburban Sonnet: Boxing Day', 'Burning Sappho', 'The Wine is Drunk'; 'someone's kindly, forgiving aunt': in Andrew Sant, *The Hallelujah Shadow: Essays* (Puncher & Wattmann: Waratah NSW, 2020) 73.

'Blue-stocking'—'a blue-stocking with an itch for scribbling': attributed to 'Pope or Gay' in Virginia Woolf, *A Room of One's Own* (Harcourt Brace & Company: New York, 1989) 61; Walter Lehmann, Francis Geyer and Timothy Kline were male pseudonyms used by Gwen Harwood.

'Burning Sappho'—Harwood: 'Burning Sappho'; 'rather be a bag lady' in Gregory Kratzmann (ed.), *A Steady Storm of Correspondence: Selected letters of Gwen Harwood 1943–1995* (UQP: St Lucia Qld, 2001) 453.

CHILDREN

Harwood: 'Return of the Native'; Scott: 'Return of the Native', 'Return to Tockington', 'Fruits of Exile'

'Her father's house'—Harwood: 'Return of the Native'

'Children'—Harwood: 'Dialogue'; Scott: 'Daughters'

'Fruits of exile'—Scott: 'Fruits of Exile': 'I serve up meals of lifeless schoolroom stuff'.

LEAVING

Harwood: 'In the Park', 'Later Texts'

MISOGYNY

Scott: 'The Witch (1)', 'The Witch (2)'

'Mending'—Scott: 'Mending a Dress'

'The other world'—Scott: 'The Witch (1)'

ALIENATION

Harwood: 'Nightfall', 'At the Arts Club', 'Monday', 'Academic Evening', 'A Music Lesson', 'The Silver Swan'

'Her grandmother'—Harwood: 'Prize-Giving', 'A Scattering of Ashes'

'Musician'—Harwood: 'The Silver Swan', 'Afternoon', 'Wind'

'Piano'—'When I married and came to Tasmania my life as a practising musician came to an end. I became a passive listener ... [it] soothed my feelings of exile' in Robert Sellick (ed.), *Gwen Harwood* (Centre for Research in the New Literatures in English: Adelaide, 1987) 4.

'Collected Poems'—'recording my familiar reminiscences while trying to slip in a few double octaves' in Gregory Kratzmann (ed.), *A Steady Storm of Correspondence: Selected letters of Gwen Harwood 1943–1995* (UQP: St Lucia Qld, 2001) 447. The last two lines echo the acrostic Harwood inserted in 'Eloisa to Abelard' and 'Abelard to Eloisa' published in *The Bulletin* in 1961 under the pseudonym Walter Lehmann: 'So long *Bulletin*, fuck all editors'.


DOMESTICITY

Scott: 'Housewife', 'Tea Party', 'Making Redcurrant Jelly', 'Polishing the Step', 'Doing the Washing'; Harwood: 'Burning Sappho'

'Marriage'—Harwood: '1945'

# Afterword

This work began life as the 'creative component' of a larger work: the thesis for which I was awarded a Doctor of Philosophy (Creative Arts and Creative Writing) degree from the University of Canberra in 2023. In that thesis entitled 'Fruits of Exile: Post-war publication of Australian female poets' I identified 'literary exile' as a metaphor for the situation of female poets confronting the male-dominated poetry establishment in Australia in the period from the 1940s to 1990s. I examined how female poets were published in literary journals and in anthologies, the publication of their individual collections and the critical response to those collections at a time when the overwhelming majority of poetry editors, anthologists, advisors to publishers and reviewers were male.

My research revealed that, for instance, in 1970 for all eight of the major literary journals less than 20% of the poets published were female, despite evidence that female poets were submitting work at a much higher rate (up to 40% of submissions). Major anthologies published in the 1960s and 1970s also included less than 20% female poets, some as low as 8%. In the period 1955–80, the eleven major publishers of Australian poetry produced 463 individual collections with just over 20% being for female poets; three of those publishers only published one female poet in that period. When collections by female poets were reviewed by male poets they commonly used derogatory labels like 'poetess', 'blue-stocking' and 'lady poet' and referred to an unfamiliar 'feminine sensibility'.

I identified a small group of influential male poets who had considerable power over other poets' legacies through their multiple, concurrent positions as poetry editors, anthologists, advisers to publishers, reviewers, academics and members of the Commonwealth Literary Fund advisory board and later the Literature Board, advising on the subsidisation of poetry collections and the award of individual grants.

As exemplars, I show how two Tasmanian poets, Gwen Harwood and Margaret Scott, dealt with their 'literary exile'. Harwood used a number of male pseudonyms to submit her poems to journals and anthologies and also nurtured friendships with at least six of the influential male poets through frequent correspondence. Similarly, Scott used her academic position at the University of Tasmania to make connections with two male poets in this group. I identify in the poetry of Harwood and Scott a strong theme of exile: their physical exile resulting from their relocation to Hobart (from Brisbane and Cambridge respectively) and their intellectual exile resulting from their domestic roles.

This volume explores how seven fictional women respond to the poetry of Harwood and Scott on the theme of exile. There are extracts from their book group discussion and poems about each of the women which reveal their own physical or metaphorical exile, whether enforced or voluntary, in the past or contemporary, and whether domestic alienation, separation from parents or from children, widowhood or leaving an abusive or unsatisfactory relationship.

# Acknowledgements

I am grateful to the many people who supported me while writing these poems and completing my PhD, including my supervisors Paul Hetherington and Jen Webb, and friends Margaret Innes, Chesley Engram, Michael Piggott and Stephen Yorke. I thank Stephanie Haygarth, Matthew Higgins, Deirdre Hyslop, Gabrielle Hyslop and Geoffrey Borny for facilitating readings of my work-in-progress and my daughters Kate and Alex Shapley for their constant support. And many thanks to Shane Strange of Recent Work Press for once again publishing my work.

'Fifty ways' was first published in Steve Meyrick (ed.), *Oystercatcher One: 101 poems*, Five Islands Press, 2024 and 'Nightfall' in *Meniscus*, 13.1, 2025.

# About the author

Dr Maggie Shapley is a Canberra poet whose poems have been published in literary journals and anthologies including *The Best Australian Poetry 2004* (UQP) and the *Anthology of Australian Prose Poetry* (MUP 2020). Her first collection, *Proof*, was published by Recent Work Press in 2017. She retired as University Archivist at the Australian National University in 2018. The first draft of her new work *Fruits of Exile* was part of her PhD thesis on the publication of Australian female poets, focusing on Gwen Harwood and Margaret Scott.

www.ingramcontent.com/pod-product-compliance
Lightning Source LLC
Chambersburg PA
CBHW060410080526
44583CB00012B/519